This book belongs to

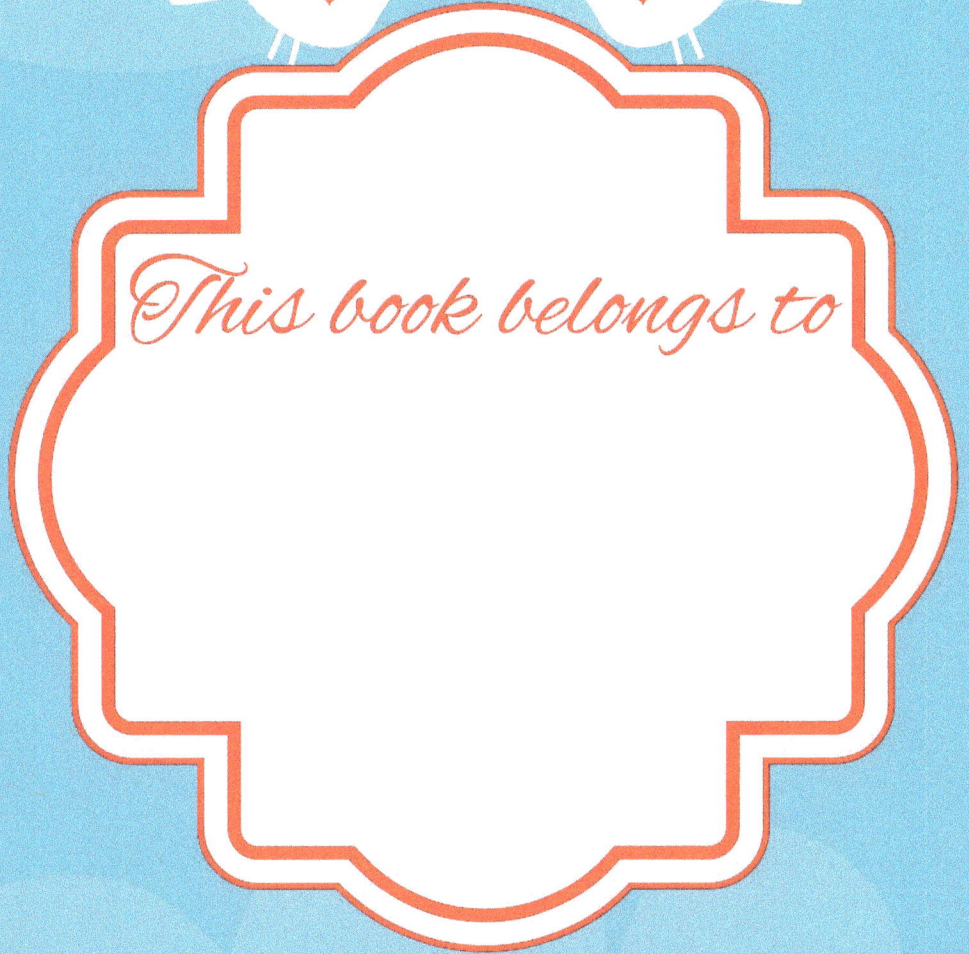

About her

Name:_____

Age and birthday:_____

Education:_____

Occupation:_____

Favourites:_____

_____

_____

_____

Hobbies:_____

_____

_____

_____

Dreams and goals:_____

_____

_____

_____

Characteristics:_____

_____

_____

_____

About him

Name:_____

Age and birthday:_____

Education:_____

Occupation:_____

Favourites:_____

_____

_____

_____

Hobbies:_____

_____

_____

_____

Dreams and goals:_____

_____

_____

Characteristics:_____

_____

_____

_____

Her family

Grandfather

Grandmother

Mother

Father

Siblings

Siblings

Siblings

Siblings

Aunts

Aunts

Aunts

Aunts

Uncles

Uncles

Uncles

Uncles

Cousins

Cousins

Cousins

Cousins

His family

Grandfather

Grandmother

Mother

Father

Siblings

Siblings

Siblings

Siblings

Aunts

Aunts

Aunts

Aunts

Uncles

Uncles

Uncles

Uncles

Cousins

Cousins

Cousins

Cousins

Photos of her

Place photo here

Place photo here

Photos of her

Place photo here

Place photo here

Photos of her

Place photo here

Place photo here

Photos of her

Place photo here

Place photo here

Photos of him

Place photo here

Place photo here

Photos of him

Place photo here

Place photo here

Photos of him

Place photo here

Place photo here

Photos of him

Place photo here

Place photo here

How we first met

How we first met

What She Wants

_____

_____

_____

_____

_____

_____

_____

_____

_____

What He Wants

Keeping it halal

Falling in love is so exciting; your heart beats like it never has before. You want to be with your partner 24/7 and get to know everything about them. You dream of romantic outings and can't wait to be together in privacy. So how do you keep it pleasing to Allah with all those emotions raging through you? Even though you may have promised to marry each other, until you actually do, you need to be aware of the boundaries. You should not be together alone without someone who acts as a "mahram" for both of you. For example, the brother or father of the prospective bride. And when you talk to each other via phone or text you need to be conscious of the language used. You can still express emotions for each other but not in ways that would cross the boundaries. Nothing you wouldn't want your parents overhearing :) .

So now you're probably thinking but where is the fun and romance in that? First of All, you need to be 100% in your heart that whatever you give up for the sake of Allah, Allah will give you something better. How many times have you heard of people saying happy/romantic marriages only last as long as the honey moon or at best a couple of years until kids show up. I'm sure you've heard it a lot and probably said to yourself but I will be different and my marriage will be filled with romance and love.

If you really want to have a marriage filled with love, happiness and romance for years to come then you really need to make sure you're pleasing Allah in the early stages before marriage and here is why:

1- If you want to be sure you're making the right decision by choosing the partner you did then you need to keep the devil's influences at a minimum. The devil can make the ugly look beautiful and he may cause you to miss signs sent to you by Allah that something is not right.

Keeping it halal

2- It's human nature to be very excited about something before they get it but after they do, they get used to it and at many times it doesn't hold the same value in their heart any more. To stop this happening in your marriage, you need Allah's continuous blessings and what best way to do that other than pleasing Allah in all your actions. Make it your intention that you will do your up most best to keep things pleasing to Him before marriage so Allah bestows His mercy on you after marriage.

3- Marriage is hard work. It's easy to fall in love before marriage but to keep that love going and strong it needs a lot of continuous hard work. So don't make it harder on yourself by starting off with loads of sins. The more blessings you have in your marriage the easier it will be for you to keep that love alive and well.

4- One of the best ways to keep couples and families together is worshipping Allah together. There will be hard times in any relationship and the devil will be making continuous efforts to break it up. But it will be much harder for the devil to have any effect if you both bring each other closer to Allah. You will also develop a deeper, more sincere kind of love that never goes away, a love that is for the sake of Allah. Not only will you love each other more but Allah willing it will also be a reason for you to enter paradise together.

Do not be fooled by romantic movies or what is shown in the media. In more cases than not it is just all a show and what happens behind the scenes is very ugly. It is not reality and it does not last. You may feel it's hard to implement, but it will only be for a very short period of time compared to spending the rest of your lives together. You need Allah now in your life more than ever, so make sure not to turn your back on Him and Allah willing, you will live a wonderful marriage life full of love and compassion.

Our Engagement

Place photo here

Place photo here

Our Engagement

Place photo here

Place photo here

Our Engagement

Place photo here

Place photo here

Our Engagement

Place photo here

Place photo here

Our Engagement

Place photo here

Place photo here

Our Engagement

Place photo here

Place photo here

Family & Friends Thoughts

Family & Friends Thoughts

Engagement memories

Engagement memories

Our Qiran Ceremony

Place photo here

Place photo here

Our Qiran Ceremony

Place photo here

Place photo here

Our Qiran Ceremony

Place photo here

Place photo here

Our Qiran Ceremony

Place photo here

Place photo here

Our Qiran Ceremony

Place photo here

Place photo here

Our Qiran Ceremony

Place photo here

Place photo here

Family & Friends Thoughts

Family & Friends Thoughts

Qiran Ceremony memories

Qiran Ceremony memories

The wedding.. A night to remember

It's a night that many girls will dream about as early as the age of 5 . It's a night that parents long to organize for their children. It signifies the start of a new life and a new journey and all the happiness that comes with it. It can also be a source of stress and family pressure if everyone is not on the same page. And unfortunately, it can be full of sins.

Since this is the start of a big journey to come, it would be much wiser if it was full of blessings from Allah. That doesn't mean that it can't be a source of joy as well, and a wonderful memory. If you want a joyful wedding full of blessings then try implementing the following points:

1- For the bride, you don't have to disobey Allah to look your best. If you want to show your hair and put on full make up then you can have separate venues for the men and women. If your wedding venue is mixed then make sure not to reveal your hair. There are many dresses out there that you can wear and you will be no less of a princess.

2- Try your best to not cave into the pressure of using a musical band or have songs played. You can hire an Islamic band that sings anasheeds using the drums. You can play different anasheeds in the background or Islamic songs.

3- Make your wedding non traditional. You can have it in an open garden or on a beach instead of a hall to avoid the music playing.

4- Ask your friends from each side to come up with some fun activities / segments they can do which are fun and halal.

The wedding.. A night to remember

5- Try not to be excessive in your wedding spending because at the end of the day it's only one night and the money could be spent in better ways, such as a wonderful honeymoon you both can remember.

6- Make the intention that you are following the tradition of the prophet "peace be upon him" in making a "waleemah" (offering food to people) for the wedding. Try to eliminate food waste by making set meals instead of open buffets.

7- It would be nice if the bride and groom could go around to each person who attended their wedding and thank them for their presence. It will also take up time and be a lovely personal touch.

8- Make sure when you get home to pray two rakath together to start your life filled with Allah's blessings.

9- Make sure to talk to your family about your expectations for the wedding and what you want. It can be difficult to convince them if they are determined in their ways but don't give up easily especially if it's about pleasing Allah. Try your best and pray to Allah to soften their hearts.

Our Wedding

Place photo here

Place photo here

Our Wedding

Place photo here

Place photo here

Our Wedding

Place photo here

Place photo here

Our Wedding

Place photo here

Place photo here

Our Wedding

Place photo here

Place photo here

Our Wedding

Place photo here

Place photo here

Family & Friends Thoughts

Family & Friends Thoughts

Family & Friends Thoughts

Family & Friends Thoughts

Wedding memories

Wedding memories

10 tips on how to win your husband's heart

Before we get started let us as wives remind ourselves of one very important fact, our husbands are our ticket to paradise insha'Allah

Al-Tirmidhi Hadith 3254 Narrated by Anas ibn Malik

Allah's Messenger (saws) said, "When a woman observes the five times of prayer, fasts during Ramadan, preserves her chastity and obeys her husband, she may enter by any of the gates of Paradise she wishes."

Al-Tirmidhi Hadith 286 Narrated by Umm Salamah

The Prophet (saws) said: "If a woman dies while her husband was pleased with her, she will enter Paradise."

So keeping the husband happy not only makes us happy, but insha'Allah will make Allah happy with us too. So how do we please our husbands? Here are some key points to keep in mind:

1- Respect. More than anything else men wish to be respected by their wives. Respect has many forms such as obeying his wishes, talking in a decent manner (even when angry :)), avoiding arguing.

2- Admiration. Men want to feel they are admired by their wives in all ways. Do not be too shy to tell him how good he looks or how clever he is. Make him feel you only have eyes for him and that you think the world of him.

3- Appreciation. Show your appreciation to what he does for you and the family on a daily basis. Do not take his working outside the house and providing for you for granted. Thank him and express your gratitude for his hard work.

4- Love him the way that pleases him. It is very important to show your husband how much you love him. Men want reassurance in this matter just as much as women do. But also make sure you do it in ways that pleases your husband. You may want to be shown love in a way that your husband dislikes and vice versa. It's not enough to do the right thing, we need to do the right thing right :)

5- Obedience. For some women this can be a sticky topic but it need not to be. Allah knows His creation more than anyone else can ever. Allah made us in certain ways and He knows what each of us men and women need to be happy. Allah has made the structure of the family that the man is the head of the household and the wife should obey her husband (of course not in anything that is against Allah's commands). The beautiful thing about it, is that Allah has made that the source of happiness and peace in the house AND a source of reward for the wife. Allah knows that women are more sentimental and more emotionally patient than men. And Allah knows that we can perform this task even though it may be difficult at times.

When you are facing a difficult situation when you have to swallow your pride and maybe anger :) know that you are doing it for Allah's sake and that it is your fight in this life and insha'Allah your key to paradise. This hadith is a great reflection on that matter:

In a Hadeeth on the authority of Ibn 'Abbaas may Allaah be pleased with him it was mentioned that a woman came to the Prophet, sallallaahu `alayhi wa sallam (may Allaah exalt his mention), and said, "O Messenger of Allaah, I am a delegate [from a group of] women and there are none of them, whether she knows or does not know that I would come to you, except she would want me to come to you. Allah The Almighty is the Lord of both men and women and their God, and you are the Messenger of Allah, for both men and women. Allah has prescribed Jihaad for men only; if they are victorious, their reward is great, and if they die as martyrs, they are alive with their Lord, receiving sustenance. [For women], which act of obedience is equal in reward to this?" The Messenger of Allaah, sallallaahu `alayhi wa sallam (may Allah exalt his mention), replied: "Obeying their husbands and (being aware of and) fulfilling their rights; and few of you do that."[At-Tabaraani and 'Abdul-Raaziq]

Here, the Messenger of Allaah, sallallaahu `alayhi wa sallam (may Allah exalt his mention), equated the reward of making Jihaad to that of the wife obeying her husband.

6- Taking care of yourself. This is VERY important and can't be stressed enough. Especially in the world we live in today and the seductions men are faced with on a daily basis. You need to take care of your looks and beautify yourself for your husband every day as much as possible. You need to try your up most best to maintain your physical appearance. It deeply affects the relationship between husband and wife. Do not fool yourself with statements like my husband should love me either way. Yes it is true that love is much deeper than appearances and a husband should love his wife either way. However, there is human nature that we can't and shouldn't ignore. Men are attracted to beautiful women so as a wife you should do your up most best that your husband has no reason to be attracted to anyone but you. Wear nice clothes each day (inside the house), put perfume on, do your make up and try to keep your weight in check. It's hard for women to maintain their weight especially after childbirth and aging and sometimes it can only be done by always watching what you consume and exercise.

But if you do put in the effort you will be rewarded for it and you will have a happier marriage, not to mention the health benefits you yourself will enjoy.

7- Balance your many tasks. As a wife and mother insha'Allah you will have many tasks to take care of and all of them are of paramount importance. You need to take care of the management of the house, the cooking (most of the time   ), cleaning, the bringing up of your children, yourself, your husband, your faith and relationship with Allah...etc. One of the best things you can do when it comes to all of these responsibilities is finding balance. For example, if you're home all day it can be very easy to get caught up in cleaning, so much so that you don't spend quality time with your children. Or you may get so caught up in taking care of all your household duties that you neglect your spiritual state. It's important you try and find a balance and try to make sure that everything takes its share. Insha'Allah you can read some tips on how to find your balance and organize your time later in the book.

8- Do not burden your husband with more than he can bear. This is especially true when it comes to financing. One of the best things you can do as a wife and will be very appreciated by your husband is to live within your means. Do not burden him with requests that will make him feel inadequate as a husband and a man. Men are very sensitive to these issues even if they are not verbal about it. Insha'Allah you can read some tips on how to be wise with your budgeting later on in the book.

9- Share his interests. While many women may find it hard to get excited about football , boxing, fishing...or whatever other manly interest your husband is into, it's very important to show interest in what your husband likes at least some of the time. Love dynamics change in a marriage with time and a big part of marriage success will rely on the friendship between the spouses. Laughing together, sharing interests and helping each other are all keys to keep the friendship strong.

10- Strengthen your relationship with Allah. The closer you get to Allah, the more the people around you including your husband will love you. You will have a light in you that surpasses any physical beauty, it will attract the people around you to your true beauty. Allah will always be there for you, pray to Him always and ask Him in your prayers to instill love in your husband's heart for you and to help you please him.

How to build a happy home

Our ultimate goal in life no matter how much we differ is essentially the same. We all want to be happy and that's the driving force of everything we do. The same applies when we are building our homes and our families. But even though it's our main desire, it's not always easy to achieve. We can't guarantee what our circumstances will be like, but we can work towards happiness regardless of what's happening around us. To have happy families we first need to be happy ourselves. We need to feel content, fulfilled and satisfied. It's easy to recognize our bodily needs and fulfil them, but we often neglect our souls. Because of that we may have everything in the worldly sense but still feel sad and depressed. We need to work on our souls individually then work together as a family to achieve happiness and peace in our hearts. Tips on how we can achieve this:

1- Our soul only finds true happiness in connecting with Allah. As individuals we need to connect with Allah on a daily basis. We need to feel His presence in our lives and seek His pleasure in everything we do. Figure out the types of worship that move your heart and bring you closer to Allah and make a schedule to implement them in your daily life.

2- Set up family gatherings where you can help each other in your worship and your connection with Allah. A family that worships Allah together; stays together.

3- Lay out goals for yourself as an individual to get closer to Allah and a plan to achieve them. After that, come together as a family and set up family goals that the younger generation can relate to, live by and carry on themselves.

4- Make sure to keep the devil's influence at a minimum. Recite Quran in your house on a daily basis. Say constant prayers to seek Allah's protection from the devil and the evil eye. Keep evil sins out of your house as much as possible such as watching inappropriate TV or listening to music. Keep your house clean of gossip and bad mouthing others.

5- Pray for your family members constantly. And make sure to use to the power of dua'a that Allah keeps you together as a happy family.

6- Try and do specific worships together such as: praying fajr together (the men can pray sunnah in the home then head to the mosque), fasting sunnah days together, reading Quran together, learning tajweed together, listening to lectures together ...etc.

7- A wonderful worship that was highly encouraged in the Quran and by the prophet Mohammed (peace be upon him) was the night prayer. If you can, try and pray at least 2 rakkath together in the middle of the night, before fajr, or even before you sleep. The last third of the night is extra special because Allah descends to the heaven of the earth and listens to the calls of His slaves and answers their prayers. Imagine if you continually asked Allah to preserve your family at that time. Allah willing, He will answer your prayers and keep you safe and happy. And most of all, don't forget to ask Allah to bring your family together in Jannat Al Firdaus (the highest place in heaven).

10 tips on how to win your wife's heart

Winning your wife's heart will not only bring you happiness on a daily basis but with the right intention it can also be a way for you to enter paradise insha'Allah. By reflecting on the following hadiths you can see that the best of men are those who treat their wives best and the best of role models in that is the prophet Mohammed (peace be upon him).

The Prophet (saws) said: 'Among the Muslims the most perfect, as regards his faith, is the one whose character is excellent, and the best among you are those who treat their wives well.' Al-Tirmidhi Hadith 628 Narrated by Abu Hurayrah Allah's Messenger (saws) said, "The best of you is he who is best to his family, and I am the best among you to my family." Al-Tirmidhi Hadith 3252   Narrated by Aisha; Abdullah ibn Abbas

The Prophet, blessings and peace be upon him, said, "The world is delightful and its greatest treasure is a good woman". (Transmitted by Muslim on the authority of Abdullah Ibn Amr (1467)

So let's get down to it, 10 tips on how to keep the wife happy

1- Safety. Women are very vulnerable creatures and constantly crave reassurance. Above anything else they always want to be sure of their value to their husbands and that nothing will ever change that. You make her feel safe by reassuring to her how much you love her and never threaten her or give her any reason to make her feel jealous.

2- Being sensitive with her emotions. Understanding that women are very emotional is key in dealing with them. The most beautiful thing about a woman is her emotions and at the same time it may seem difficult to deal with. Women can often cry with no apparent reason or worse they can cry even if they are happy   . Logic at these times often doesn't work and the best policy is just to be there for your wife. A cuddle, a kiss, an attentive ear and I'm here for you is all she needs.

3- Appreciation. Wives have a lot on their plate and a lot to deal with. While husbands are usually mainly occupied with what is going on at work, wives have to deal with all household issues, taking care of the husband and children and a lot of the time work as well. You will find that just simple words of appreciation will make her full of joy and will give her all the energy she needs to cope with her tasks. In fact she may even surprise you and often go the extra mile please you even further.

4- Romance. Most men are not that romantic especially after marriage but often the opposite is true with women. They crave romance and it never really goes away. Even if it's once a year, make her feel like a princess. Take her out to dinner on candle light, get her flowers, write her a beautiful card,...etc.

10 tips on how to win your wife's heart

Tell her you love her. Many men find it hard to express their emotions verbally and often think it is not necessary. But in fact it is very important to women, it is not enough that you show it but women also needs to hear it. You will be surprised at how simply saying "I love you" can make her very happy and reflect on her overall behavior.

5- Respect. While women can often cope with more than men can emotionally and are more accepting in general, they still want to be respected and taken in high regard. Women may not voice their hurt from disrespect but it will definitely hurt them and it will come out in other ways. Treat her as you would like to be treated yourself.

6- Help around the house. If you want to score points in no time then this is the way to go. Even if it's just a few simple tasks that you can help with around the house, it will mean the world to her. Don't forget to also put an intention that you are following the prophet's (peace be upon him) example in this.

7- Compliments. Women love compliments, especially from their husbands. And especially about their looks   . Women are emotional beings and loving compliments are often all they need to feel happy and content.

8- Help her reach her maximum potential. Standing by your wife and helping her achieve her dreams and goals in life will make her put you in very high regard. Not only will she love you more for it but by her being happy it will help you both have a happier marriage.

9- Encourage her to get closer to Allah. Husbands have a very big role in bringing the whole family closer to Allah. The more you care about your relationship with Allah and the more you help your wife get closer to Allah too the more she will love you and appreciate you. Be merciful with her and help her learn more about her religion. This is one of your main responsibilities and not only will it win your wife's heart, you will also be rewarded for it.

10- Be her friend. Treat her like your best friend. Ask her opinion on matters concerning you, women love to help and offer support. Spend time with her doing things that preferably you both enjoy. Talk with her, joke with her and share your life with her. Being her friend also requires that you listen to her, while paying attention   . Generally women talk much more than men do and while you may not want to talk as much as she does, you can still listen. She will feel valued, appreciated and you will both have a happier healthier marriage for it.

Our Family Goals

Our Family Goals

True love

Before marriage our idea about love is mostly from romantic movies and novels. Unfortunately, the picture is somewhat skewed and can have a negative effect later on if we don't let go of it. It's not that love doesn't exist after marriage; in fact it's the total opposite. A lot of the time the love we feel before marriage is mixed with immaturity and lust. After marriage our loves transforms into something much more deep and meaningful.

True love is about sacrifice, its about loving your partner after you know their faults and you choose to love them regardless. It's about getting angry and frustrated at times but having the power to forgive. It's about showing your love day in and day out. If you feel the love is dwindling in your marriage life, try some of these tips:

1- Give without taking. Make the decision that you will take action to increase the love in your marriage regardless of the outcome. Fix yourself and do your part, you will definitely see the rewards even if down the track.

2- Do something nice for your partner without an occasion. Buy them a present, write them a letter, even if you just give them a hug and thank them for being in your life.

3- Don't sweat the small stuff. Try to look at the big picture and don't get caught up with little things that can end into needless fights and hurt emotions. Criticism can be very destructive even if done with good intentions. It can make the person feel unappreciated and unloved.

4- Always show your appreciation. Nothing can kill a marriage faster than lack of appreciation from either side. Appreciate everything no matter how small and make sure to show it.

True love

5- Be patient and forgiving. Things will happen that will upset and hurt you. You will get annoyed and frustrated. Be the bigger one and let it go. Make excuses for your partner. I'm sure if you look closer you will find they are dealing with their own stuff. Maybe they are under immense pressure, maybe they are feeling insecure..etc. We are all human and we will inevitably mess up. Just be patient as much as you can and it will pass.

6- Make sure to always have a smile on your face. No matter how bad things get , don't forget to smile. Life after marriage and especially kids changes a lot. You will have more responsibilities than ever and time will just slip past. Even a small smile in the midst of the storm can give the necessary reassurance and care for the love to grow.

7- Don't believe everything you read. If you're on social media a lot you will see countless examples of couples announcing their eternal love for each other. If you're having a bad day it can cause you pain and make you feel annoyed with your partner and marriage. The thing is everyone has their struggles and more times than not those who display their emotions in front of the world are the ones who are struggling the most. People tend to show only the good side but the times they were on the brink of divorce are never showed. So you will be fooled to think that it's all fun and joy when reality is far from that.

8- Don't share your problems with the world. What happens in your house should stay in your house unless there is a critical situation that needs to be addressed. Families can tend to be biased and if their interference sometimes can cause more harm than good. Friends can have good intentions but they can easily be misleading with their advice. Always try to please Allah when solving any issues and Allah will make it easy for you.

What I love about her

What I love about him

Our Honeymoon

Place photo here

Place photo here

Our Honeymoon

Place photo here

Place photo here

Our Honeymoon

Place photo here

Place photo here

Our Honeymoon

Place photo here

Place photo here

Our Honeymoon

Place photo here

Place photo here

Our Honeymoon

Place photo here

Place photo here

Honeymoon memories

Honeymoon memories

Special Memories

Special Memories

Special Memories

Special Memories

Special Memories

Special Memories

Special Memories

Special Memories

Special Memories

Special Memories

Halah Azim
Our story

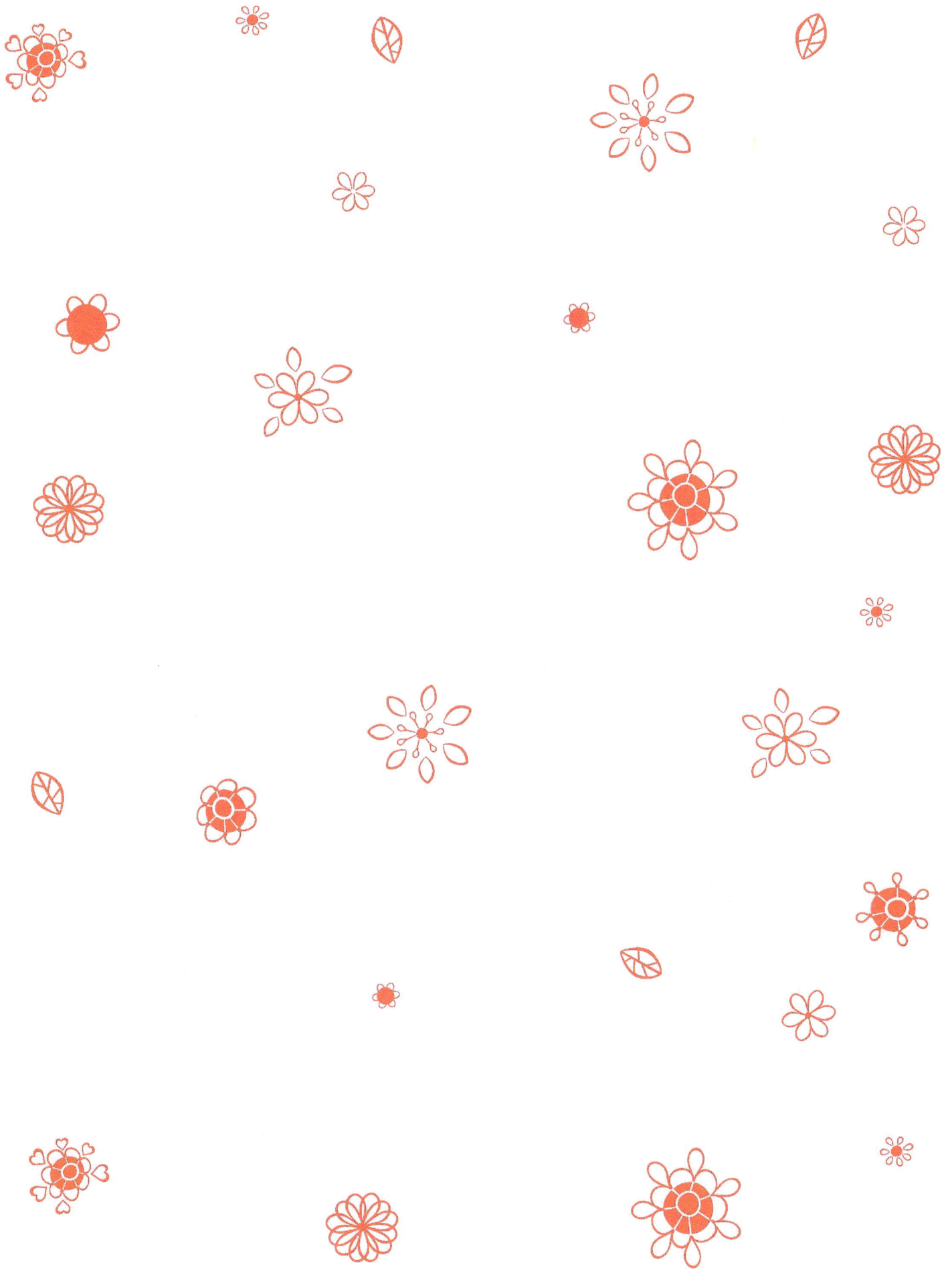